WEEKS IN THIS COUNTRY

# WEEKS
# IN THIS
# COUNTRY

*Vivé Griffith*

*The Kent State University Press*

*Kent, Ohio, and London*

Library of Congress Catalog Card Number 00-0000
ISBN 0-87338-662-0
Manufactured in the United States of America

07  06  05  04  03  02  01  00    5  4  3  2  1

The Wick Poetry Chapbook Series is sponsored by the Stan and Tom Wick
Poetry Program and the Department of English at Kent State University.

Library of Congress Cataloging-in-Publication Data
Griffith, Vivé, 1968–
    Weeks in this country / Vivé Griffith.
        p.      cm.—(Wick poetry chapbook series two; no. 7)
    ISBN 0-87338-662-0 (pbk.: alk paper) ∞
    I. Title.    II. Wick poetry chapbook series; ser. 2, no. 7.

PS3557.R52 W44    2000
811'.54—dc21                                                    99-051695

British Library Cataloging-in-Publication data are available.

*For my mother,*
*for making me promise*
*the first book would be hers*

CONTENTS

Longing, we say, because desire is full
of endless distances.

—Robert Hass

ACKNOWLEDGMENTS

Grateful acknowledgment is made to the publications in which earlier versions of the following poems appeared or will appear: "*Le Baiser De l'Hôtel De Ville,* Forty Years Later," *Black Warrior Review,* under the title "Forty Years After *Le Baiser De l'Hôtel De Ville*"; "Letter to Maureen from Turkey" and "Late Night Longings," *Malahat Review;* "Weeks in This Country," *Spoon River Poetry Review.*

I have been fortunate to work with people whose generosity and attention to my poetry have enriched this collection and my work overall. Special thanks to my professors Don Bogen, John Drury, Andrew Hudgins, and Ellen Bryant Voigt; to Maggie Anderson; and to my peers Stephen Frech, Maureen Ryan Griffin, Dede Mitchell, Jim Murphy, Cynthia Nitz Ris, and Adam Sol, among many others, for challenging me and encouraging me. What a gift to know people who listen for, in the words of Seamus Heaney, "the music of what happens."

## LETTER TO MAUREEN FROM TURKEY

Hello friend. Today it was Ankara,
where the women wear cropped tops
and couples drink beer at sidewalk cafés.
That's not what makes me write to you.
At the museum I lingered before a clay fertility goddess
captured in a glass case. She was all
breasts and thighs, all woman,
and there she was, eight thousand years later,
still giving birth, still bearing down
in the way, you'd tell me, women create the world.
Kids are everywhere—everywhere—
in this country. I saw a boy climb the *mimbar*
while his father, praying, touched his forehead
to the ground. Another threw Coke cans in the fountain.
The Ottoman citadel's narrow streets
pulsed with children peddling
scarves embroidered by their mothers
and hand-made lace. A girl named Kemal
held my hand, her fingers fit so easily in mine,
and led me around loose stones
to the top. Paused
above scattered timber roofs and pastel walls,
I could almost trust in stasis, a pristine world.
How did you do it—sign on
for what they call the full catastrophe—
the husband, the children, the solid brick home?
The world isn't pristine, and my trust in it
as flimsy as a cigar-smoking old man's.
You know the type, slumped on a bus,
muttering *What is the world coming to?*
And kids are everywhere.
Did I mention Kemal's eyes were dark like mine?
She wore faded jeans and her haggling, well,
it was refined. In the midst of disillusionment

the world calls for such acts of faith.
You have yours in Amanda and Dan.
I have a new hotel, where neon flashes
outside the window like I'm trapped
in a film noir. Even these travels,
these endless travels, can't be as simple
as Roman ruins and apricots spilling in markets.
The fertility goddess is a postcard
and I couldn't help buying Kemal's lace.

## MY FATHER'S WEDDING

The invitation came one Saturday morning,
his handwriting on the envelope. Inside:
*Para descubrir nuestro maravilloso mundo . . .*
and his name, misspelled.

•

When I visited three years ago
she was the maid
who served him black coffee every morning,
washed clothes in a basin on the front porch.
We traveled to Santo Domingo
and he brought her back a satin blouse.

She gave up her bed for me, slept on a cot in his room.

•

He married her in the *campo,*
where each family keeps chickens and pigs
and meals are cooked over open flames
in the huts behind houses.

He sent me the pictures.
They pose against a backdrop of lace and balloons,
the shingles of faded blue wood
barely showing above the fringe.

•

Gauguin painted and painted again
his island wife
until she was no longer bare feet and dark skin,
but Mary, Eve, every woman.

Would I rather there had been bright sarongs,
a yellow sky, blue trees?

.

Her own father once shimmied a tall palm
to bring us coconuts. As he lifts his glass
for a champagne toast, he doesn't smile.

.

White plastic tables under a purple canopy,
a colonnade of palm fronds,
a two-tiered cake.

He'd planned it
for Thanksgiving week,
but confused the date.

.

Why mention that she is younger than me?
Why wonder about the strangers
who crowd in around them?
Why wish him anything else?

He sent me the pictures
as if to say, *This is real.*

## WINTER MORNING

You sing in the shower. I sip hot tea
and stare at barren trees and dirty snow,
wishing us back to Rome—an open window,
saxophone music, the sway of our bodies.
I'd meet you again at piazza Navona,
near women peeling artichokes. We'd have hours
of talk, paintings by Balla, and the sweet blur
of pausing to kiss on the via Bogogna.
You say last night you woke to find the room
illumined, almost alive. You didn't speak,
just watched as the angles of my face were hewn
by light. I lay lost in dreams where I seek
other places, unaware of the stroke of the moon,
the rhythm of your breath on my cheek.

# THE MAN WHO LEANS

The man in the photograph leans against a tree
in front of a boarded-up tower.
It is another country. It doesn't matter where.
On the ground around his boots, soggy brown leaves
and bits of discarded paper. He leans
as if he is all about leaning.
The slope, the tilt, is everything.

The man who leans has stories
his lean would never tell.
The vinyl bag slung across his shoulder
once belonged to a Finnish dentist.
He tried to know the man through a daughter's stories,
through letters of condolence in a language
he couldn't read. On a train platform,
he kissed that daughter without promises,
leaning on her certainty, on the distant rumble of tracks.

The man who leans trusts he'll be supported.
He doesn't need memories or photos of his family—
there's Heidegger in his bag,
a sketch book with battered edges.
The old, leafless tree is enough.
The camera, set on a timer, enough.

He doesn't ask what's to come—
what city, what corduroy-wearing stranger,
what next after the flight home.
He's the moment he wants to live in,
the moment he knows he exists in.
The tree's damp bark
not yet worked through to his shoulder.

# LETTER FROM PRAGUE, 1994

> To be an artist means
> never to avert one's eyes.
> —Akira Kurosawa

They don't stand in line for bread anymore,
but the habit of shoving dies hard,
and I feel always jostled.

It's been two years since you signed your book
*To a Sister Poet.* That word—poet—
more real in your felt tip than any place
in my life, hinged on something I couldn't name.
I decided there, that night, I wanted to be you.

Now home is a flat filled with someone else's
shabby belongings. Mornings I write in a kitchen
where all the wood is painted orange,
gracious morsel of brightness
as winter sets in Prague: monochrome, polluted.
Again and again I go to American Express,
clutch my letters as I cross Wenceslas Square,
words from home assuring I'm brave, loved.

I have no political prisoners to write about,
only my Czech friend who says her grandfather
lost his home and business, was forced
into the mines and interrogated until
he died of a heart attack at fifty-two.
But that was 1969, after the Prague Spring,
the Soviet invasion, before she was born.
Her American boyfriend brushes hair
from her eyes, traces her high cheekbones.

Maybe I should have gone farther.

In Albania, houses with empty pantries
still have the television sets
where once bureaucrats tried to convince
the people that they were rich.
In Romania, I could stare in the faces of those
who would steal from me, my least precious
as valuable in their fingers
as gold once sewn in jacket linings.

Made it as far as Poland. Before I saw Auschwitz
or the barbed wire of Birkenau,
before I entered the barracks where
invisible hands seemed to push me out,
I walked the rain-drenched streets and cried.
I wanted to love Poland and the people
who rebuilt their city after Nazi tanks leveled it
street by street by street. All I felt
was smog covering me like a layer of skin.
I took the night train out.

Then I realized I don't want to be
someone else, Carolyn. Not even you.
Your poems speak of cyclone fences
and ears come alive in a glass of water.
Sometimes I can't even look
at a man passed out on the street,
his head off the curb on a sewer grate
and a violent shadow spreading across his pants.

## LATE-NIGHT LONGINGS

3 A.M. I am watching
a man in black leather
lift the pinball machine
each time the ball
is about to roll away.
I want his easy ability
to break the rules.
I want the movement
of my body to the music
to be unconscious.
I hear my mother's voice
telling me not
to touch anything.
I want to touch
everything, nothing
separating me from it.
I want to read graffiti
without needing
to write it down—
*I'm empty I'm empty*
*farted in the water*
*and made no bubbles.*
I want to be empty.
I want to sit
with this bearded man's
knee against mine
and not memorize
the shiver of my skin.
I want him to want
my smell on his body
and me not know it.
I want not to know
if I want him too.
I want smoke in my lungs,

beer on my tongue,
the pulse of the music
droning, drowning
everything out.

## MY MOTHER TAUGHT ME
## WILDFLOWERS

Wildflowers speckle these Alpine
hillsides, far from her, a place
I might have imagined those summer days
when she and I, on hands and knees,
searched for four-leaf clovers.
With their promised luck, they eluded me,
though years later I took my grandmother's
Shakespeare from a shelf and one fluttered out,
brown and whole in darkened plastic.

Pussy willows filled vases. At times
we pulled from the road at the sight
of lily-of-the-valley, my mother dropping
down, submitting to the scent.

In the city she was drawn to five o'clock
happy hours, weekends at the condo pool.
Often she left me to cultivate myself
while she drifted, a tuft of milkweed
on the breeze. I turned toward
friends who taught me to dig and pat soil,
love pansies, gladioli,
the true red of geraniums in window boxes.

I hike this trail with a Slovak friend
who picks herbs to chew or crumble for juice
to speed healing. He takes my hand and invites
me to skip, says the body can journey
long distances this way. I teach him
the English names of wildflowers—Queen Anne's lace,
clover, black-eyed Susan, dandelion.
*Yes,* I answer, *lion,* like the animal.

Wherever I look, I see them.

IN PRAGUE

This morning at the tram stop
a boy swung round and round a metal pole.
He wore blue jeans, dirty sneakers,
a fatigue baseball cap with the words

*West Point* in block letters. In his hand,
a toy pistol. It's not about children's games
anymore—no cowboys and Indians,
cops and robbers. My friend in Los Angeles

wrote to say he was chased through the streets
by gang members, the barrel of a rifle
over the dash. He escaped when traffic parted,
like a scene from the movies

he went there to study. Do I tell him
I can walk alone here after dark,
have never learned the Czech word for *help?*
On his way to school, the boy must pass

those bars where men with dark circles
under their eyes, men who know no other
life, drink vodka and *pivo* before work.
They ride steep escalators into the subway,

are ferried to factory jobs in the suburbs.
No different from the men I see stumbling
late hours through the streets. Last night,
over the pulse of pop music,

a Czech friend told me I don't need
to smile at every pause in conversation.
*If you're sad,* she said, *be sad.*
*In communist times, to ask "How are you?"*

*was to invite complaints over things not had,*
*not allowed. In communist times, America*
*shined in the distance, a place*
*where the answer was always "Fine."*

## WEEKS IN THIS COUNTRY

where women with scarved heads
and stout bodies bend over eggplant
and peppers in the market,
where they lead mules by the reins,
filling baskets with apricots,
where they stretch their hands
through iron grates in the courtyard,
and still I don't know
what they reach for, or why.

A man at the mosque hisses me
from the splendid entrance
and points to an ordinary door at the side.
My Birkenstocks slouch
next to scuffed heels and peeling vinyl
and I descend to the women's section
where there is no grandeur, just paint chipping
from walls, electrical wires lying exposed.

In a small room, two women gossip.
In another, a body draped in black faces east.
In a third, a gathering of seated women
turns toward one who sings.
Her voice, like a veil, wraps around me,
stops my leaving. The song is
my sister braiding my hair,
my mother adjusting my head covering,
with thick and gentle fingers, a friend
dropping sugar cubes into my tea—
one, two—just how I like it.

## AN AMERICAN, A CZECH,
## A HOUSE IN A VILLAGE

A fire burns in the wood stove.
The dog lies next to it
on a bed of gray blankets.

The first snow has melted
but I cannot shake the chill
from my hands and feet.

Your pockets are filled
with apples
from the tree in back.

I slice, you roll the dough.
We are one more pair
of women in a kitchen

with conversation drifting
through an afternoon
scented of cinnamon.

We could be anyone,
anywhere, in any time.
It is always the same.

The apples are spiced
and sugared.
You lift the dough

from both sides,
join it at the top
and press the seams.

## THOSE DRIFTWOOD MONTHS

The summer she waited tables in Provincetown,
my mother rented a narrow room in a boarding
house and woke with salty lips each morning.
Those driftwood months grew to myth: surrounded
by salt marsh aster, she found freedom. She might
have wished her life were only this, nothing more—
she's never said. But one day she walked the shore
and saw a woman painting at the ocean side.
It was her own mother, alone, stealing
the waves. My grandmother, whose landscapes lined
my childhood walls, drove hours to catch that bend
of light, the lazy foam of the ocean's retreating.
Both were home before the seaside lavender bloomed.
I'm left with the canvas, the story, the longing, the poem.

## THE FLIGHT HOME

The woman in the seat in front of me
tips her head back to read *Paradise of Love*
through bifocal lenses—

*jeweled, silk, glitter, lavish—*
she enters a world of long-legged women
and men who *push away memory.*

When she fixes her lipstick
in a small mirror, I see her face
is spotted with age. I am returning

from a place some have called paradise.
My legs, never *willowy,* are covered
with bug bites and the dirt

is still embedded under my nails.
I expected to find others there
in search of the poetic, the epiphytes

on ancient trees all climbing
toward the light. Instead they spoke
the language of science—

*obligate mutualism, astrogyne—*
kept species lists in their notebooks.
Or they rafted the furious rivers,

forged their own paths through
the rain forest, proving the courage
I lack. The woman turns the page:

*Except that even now he could not*
*harden his heart against her.*
Perhaps she will finish the book

after serving her husband coffee
in the breakfast nook, a bank calendar
tacked to the floral wallpaper.

I have been gone three weeks.
The man who meets me at the airport
isn't dashing, won't sweep me off

to a place where I wear *an elegant cluster
at the nape,* where rumor circles
ice sculptures that glisten at 3 A.M.

It will be quieter than that
while we try to recover
the language we hold in common.

## LE BAISER DE L'HÔTEL DE VILLE, FORTY YEARS LATER

—After the photograph by Robert Doisneau

Even Paris seemed small compared to him.
He gave me what we all dreamed of—
the breathless twirl of a man's arms
about me, the moment it all went silent,
even the roar of cars from the boulevard,
when he swept me into that kiss.
The flowers he brought were orange-red tulips.
*Fire,* he said. We love what consumes us.

Sometimes, now, he slips and calls me *Mother.*
It's natural, I suppose, with our children
and their children planted so deep in our lives.
My own name on his lips is strange.
And when I wander the city these days
I am often alone. He prefers long walks
on solitary roads, the dapple of light
through a canopy of leaves, the gift of silence.

On the noisy streets, vendors hold our image
out in black and white, try to sell what it meant
to be young and in love in Paris. I imagine
dreamy girls who hang it on their walls,
stare at it each night, murmuring *if only,*
*if only I could know one moment like that*
*the world would always be different.*
There are times when I inhale his scent
from the bedclothes before setting them to wash,
or his fingers brush my back as he passes by,
in their tips the knowing of forty years.
Those times I almost believe it too.

## TO THE SIDEWALK ARTIST

In Prague, where cracked sidewalks are littered
with shit, you offer a ten-foot square of art.
A crowd of people has gathered

around the shapes and curves, rare in this marred
landscape where decades ago spires gave way
to tenements, and hardened

women become part of the towering gray.
They drag themselves and sacks of cabbage,
potatoes, sausage, poppyseed, eggs.

The pavement before you is lavish
with color. Who remembers yellow
during an Eastern European winter awash

in monotony? While change clinks in shallow
buckets, you render the playwright
president in fluent lines, an angel crouched low

on his shoulder whispering words we might
guess at. You step back, ribbons of chalk
confusing your clothes, your creation bright

and animated on the sidewalk
where with each hour it will fade
until all that remains is a mark

in your memory. On a canvas Renoir gave
us a scene—music plays and dancers whirl
while a fair-haired figure bends to savor

conversation. A hundred years later this girl
still bends, still savors, the lace
at her throat still a smudge. But I turn

back to you making art in ephemeral places.
It's true I'll forget the image as transient as sand,
but not the careful debate of your face

or the sweep of the chalk in your hand.

## MEANWHILE, THEY MARCH
## IN BARCELONA

Red flags raised high,
banners sweeping
                    the width of the street,
men lean in to talk together

while their worn shoes move in sync
with the worn shoes of other workers.

A cloud of brown wool
on a winter's day.

        I have dreamed of the march,
have yearned for causes,
                for pilgrimages
                        made to sacred shrines.

The missionary speaking Spanish
has narrow lips,
                carefully parted hair.
His navy sweater bears no sign
        of the lint he pinched from it
in the morning's
                early hours.
                        Passing by me,

voices rising in tremulous harmony.

(When I stumbled upon a Papal audience
in St. Peter's Square,
                it wasn't the Pope
        who awed me.
It was the faces,

                thousands of faces, intent
upon his figure
                framed in scarlet curtains.)

*Una mas. Una mas.*
                Shopkeepers look
to the street, shake their heads, look
away. The missionary is from Utah
and would rather
                talk to
                        than convert me.

On this Barcelona sidewalk
                it is easy
to pretend we are from the same place.

        But I have no march
to join, no faith to swear by
                on foreign streets.

        Where do I belong
more than here,
                sliding past
unknown faces, ticket
                for the next morning's train
        dampening in my hand?

# GÖREME VALLEY

— Turkey, 1996

1.

While you sleep in the shelter
of a cave room, I look out on hills
that ripple like the soft peaks
of beaten egg whites, tufa rock
changing color in the light.
We come here not knowing
if we are beginning or ending.
Morning arrives with the frenzy
of swifts swooping and diving
from high pigeon platforms.

2.

In the cliffside, the domes and columns,
apses and naves of fifteenth-century churches,
the reds of the frescoes still true. The smell
of urine slaps us, wells for grain or wine
are littered with empty water bottles.
I lose you in the shadows.
                    You find me
staring up at the faces of Christ and the saints,
their eyes scratched out by invaders.

Later you enter the womb
of an ancient monastery, climb higher
through the vertical shafts, gripping handholds
in the walls. In the small cells, men sat alone
fingering rosaries. From the ground I see
your bead-sized face appear in a hillside window.

3.

A box of condoms,
      one missing,
half-buried in sand
      between the grape bushes.

Did they lie here
      last night,
when we saw light streak
      across a clear sky?

4.

Doğan once lived in Arizona, but returned home
to sell carpets from his grandparents' caravansary.

He searches for stories in the weavings—a prayer rug
with twin staircases leading to heaven and hell,

the pairs of birds that face one another in love
or turn away in anger. Together we choose

a multi-colored kilim, where rams' horns
and wolves' mouths protect the woman's image

repeated in the center—Anatolian
fertility goddess, hands on hips, giving birth.

5.

Across from the hotel, a couple squats
beside the apricots they've left to dry on the roof.

Her head is scarved, his arms darkened
by days in the field. They sway together
as they turn row after row. Behind them,
the sun sets saffron red, like the lentils, spices, fruits
that spill from burlap bags in the market.

6.

At night I burn with fever, as if the afternoon sun
still beats at the top of my head,
tremble, my arms and legs frozen under layers
of wool blankets. You wipe my forehead
with cool rags, pour glasses of water, finally slip

beneath the covers and press your bare body
against mine. Outside our room, rock formations
rise unchanged, solitary against the sky.